Practical Hints on playing the

ALTO CLARINET

by Arthur J. Nix
in collaboration with James D. Ployhar

Foreword

The "Practical Hints" series is a unique and highly informative set of books designed to answer the many important questions raised by the beginning musician as well as the more advanced student.

Each book has been prepared by a nationally known instrumental specialist and covers such vital topics as CARE AND MAINTENANCE, REEDS AND MOUTHPIECES, PLAYING POSITION, EMBOUCHURE, TUNING, TONGUING, TONE QUALITY and RANGE as well as the methodology of PRACTICE.

Every book contains a number of pictures along with practical playing exercises designed to rapidly improve basic musicianship.

The "Practical Hints" series may be used along with the FIRST DIVISION BAND COURSE, the CONTEMPORARY BAND COURSE or any other recognized band method. An appropriate book from this series should be in every young musicians' library as a companion book to the method.

The books in the "Practical Hints" series are for individual use only and may not be played together in a band class. Books are published separately for the following instruments:

Published for:

FLUTE	ALTO SAXOPHONE	BARITONE
Bb CLARINET	TENOR SAXOPHONE	(Euphonium)
ALTO CLARINET	BARITONE SAXOPHONE	TUBA (Bass)
BASS CLARINET	CORNET/TRUMPET	PERCUSSION (Snare Drum,
OBOE	FRENCH HORN	Bass Drum, Timpani, Cymbals)
BASSOON	TROMBONE	MALLET PERCUSSION

Belwin Mills Publishing Corp.

MELVILLE, N. Y. 11747

EL 2702

About the Author

Arthur J. Nix is a native of North Dakota. He received his undergraduate degree from Moorhead State University, Moorhead, Minnesota and his M.A. from the University of Northern Colorado, Greeley, Colorado. He was the Director of Bands at Moorhead State for twenty-three years and is continuing on the staff as single reed instructor. He is active as an adjudicator and clinician and is Alto, Bass and Contra-Bass Clarinet instructor at the International Music Camp, International Peace Gardens during the summer.

Mr. Nix has written nine solos you will be able to use in improving your playing. These solos are correlated with Books I, II, and III of the "CONTEMPORARY BAND COURSE — BAND TODAY" published by Belwin-Mills Publishing Corp. They were written to help you develop tonguing, tone quality, range and a feeling for phrasing and musical content.

A special thanks to Barbara Herbranson for typing and Marlowe Kulish for drawings.

Contents

Unit I. Care and Maintenance

A. SWABBING AND CLEANING

It is very important that the bore of the instrument be dried after being used. Swabbing removes the excess moisture from the bore of the instrument and prevents the moisture from gathering on the pads while in the case. The pads swell and deteriorate, affecting response and intonation. If the instrument is made of wood, swabbing dries the bore and helps to prevent cracking.

1. Remove bell, neck pipe and mouthpiece. Lay these parts in your case. Take the swab and drop the weighted end through the bottom section. Make sure the swab is not balled or bunched. Pull out and down on the string. Check the bore and, if more moisture is present, repeat. For two piece clarinets, pull the center section apart and dry the center receiver. Moisture will gather there. Place these sections in your case.

2. Remove the reed, dry it between the thumb and first finger. Place it in reed guard. Drop the weighted end of the swab through the large end of the mouthpiece and pull gently to dry the inside of the mouthpiece. Put the mouthpiece in a clean sock or wrap in a soft cloth and store in case. Next, dry the inside of the bell section and put in case. Next dry the neck-pipe. Once a month wash the inside of the mouthpiece. Washing removes food particles and other debris that gather in the tone chamber. Fill a wash-basin with *WARM WATER. NOT HOT!* Using *MILD SOAP* and a soft rag, wash inside and outside. *HOLD* the mouthpiece so it will not drop. Put a soft towel in the washbowl just in case. Dry the mouthpiece inside and out. Wipe the cork and apply new grease.

3. If at any time the swab becomes stuck, *DO NOT* try to remove it by poking a screwdriver or similar tool into the tone holes. There is danger of breaking a tone hole. Take the instrument to the band director and have him remove it, or he will take that section of the clarinet to an instrument repair shop where they have the proper tools to remove the swab.

B. OILING BORE AND KEYS

1. Bore — Clarinets are manufactured from two materials, wood or high impact plastic. Wooden instruments require a routine oiling of the bore. It is recommended the bore be oiled once a month. Swabs and special oil for this purpose can be purchased at a music store. Apply a few drops of oil to the swab and work in with the fingers. Push the swab into the bore, move in and out several times to leave a thin coat of oil. *DO NOT* soak the swab, as too much oil will leave a coating on the pads. When pads become oil soaked they become hard, leak and fall apart. After oiling the bore, take the swab and rub it over the outside of the instrument. Using a pipe cleaner, oil the inside of the tone holes to clean them and to prevent them from cracking. Oiling the tone holes also prevents water from collecting and producing gurgling notes. The bell, neck-pipe and mouthpiece do not need to be oiled.

2. Keys — Too often this important part of maintenance is overlooked. The clarinet has many movable parts in its key system. The keys fit between pivot posts and are held securely against the posts by pivot screws and rods running through the keys. Key oil will help reduce this friction and wear and keep the key action light, fast and positive. Key oil is available from the band director or music dealer. With a toothpick or dropper supplied in the bottle, put a drop of oil on all pivot points and posts. Press the key up and down several times to work the oil into the points of friction. When finished, wipe off the excess oil with a clean cloth. Proper oiling will prolong the life of the instrument. Nothing is more frustrating than to have a key stick or not respond fast enough when playing. When finished playing, wipe the keys with a soft cloth to remove perspiration. The keys will stay shiny.

3. Greasing — Corks need grease to keep them soft. Soft corks help keep the joints air tight and make assembling the instrument much easier. It is recommended that old grease be cleaned off the corks from time to time. Use a clean soft rag for this purpose.

4. Storing — The case has been designed to protect the different parts of the instrument. *NEVER* carry music stands, music folders or other articles in your case unless there is a special compartment for that purpose. Extra materials or objects will bend keys, spring key posts, and, in general, interfere with the proper maintenance of the instrument. Make sure the individual parts are placed in their proper compartments. To protect the mouthpiece, it is recommended that the ligature, cap and reed be removed from the mouthpiece. Place the reed in a reed guard. Place the cap and ligature in the case. Now wrap the mouthpiece in a piece of soft cloth or deposit it in a large sock, and then put it in the case. By wrapping the mouthpiece, the student is protecting the table, rails and tip from being scratched or nicked.

Unit II. Choosing the Correct Mouthpiece,
Reed and Ligature

A. MOUTHPIECES

Mouthpieces are manufactured from two materials, plastic or rubber. Plastic is less expensive but is not as stable as rubber, so it is recommended that the instrument be equipped with a good rubber mouthpiece. As this is such an important part of the instrument, it should be treated with care and respect. As mentioned in "UNIT I — CARE AND MAINTENANCE", it should be protected from scratches, nicks and chips on the tip, rails and table. Figure 1.

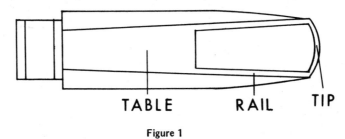

TABLE   RAIL   TIP

Figure 1

Refer to the above picture. Notice the table of the mouthpiece. It is absolutely flat. Any damage to this area will affect the seal of the reed. Next notice the rails of the mouthpiece as they travel toward the tip. See how thin they are? This is the part of the mouthpiece against which the sides of the reed vibrate. The next important part is the tip of the mouthpiece. This is the part that the tip of the reed vibrates against. Notice also that the tip of the mouthpiece is curved to fit the curve of the reed. All of these measurements are important, the length and width of the table, the length and width of the rails, and the curve and thickness of the tip. If there are any scratches, nicks or chips on these important parts, the reed will not respond properly, resulting in stuffy tones and squeaks.

On the side of the mouthpiece there will be a letter, number or combination of letters or numbers. The manufacturer uses these numbers or letters to inform the player how near or how far away the resistance curve is from the tip. See Figure 2 for resistance curve explanation. A *medium-open* mouthpiece is recommended for most students.

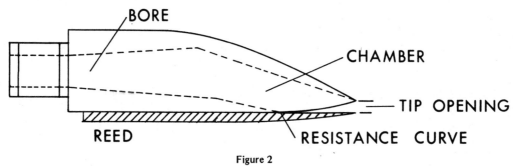

BORE

CHAMBER

TIP OPENING

REED   RESISTANCE CURVE

Figure 2

B. REEDS

Many playing problems result from a poor reed, so attention to this section will help select, adjust and store reeds. If a reed has cracks or chips in the tip or is not balanced, the tone of the instrument will be lacking in body and clarity. In addition, intonation problems, response in tonguing and squeaking may and can result. Care needs to be taken to select a good reed. Selecting the proper strength, adjusting, regulating and storing is very important to successful playing.

Reeds are graded by numbers or words. A manufacturer may use the numbers 1½, 2, 3, 4, and 5. The lower the number the softer the reed. Another manufacturer will use the words, soft, medium-soft, medium, medium-hard and hard. In either case these are approximate strengths and can be used only as a rough guide to reed strength. One must keep in mind that reeds are manufactured from cane, and cane is wood. Because cane is wood it can vary from reed to reed or from one piece of cane to the next. The best cane is grown in the southern part of France. The soil, moisture and sunlight conditions are the best for this purpose.

It is recommended that a reed strength of 1½ to 2 or soft to medium-soft be used on the larger clarinets. All too often a reed that is too hard is used on the larger clarinets. This results in a tone that is harsh, has poor response, has a tendency to be sharp in pitch and, most important, causes the student to use an embouchure that is too firm. Excess lip pressure, due to a stiff reed, filters out the mellow overtones and the warm sounds that are so characteristic of the larger clarinets.

1. SELECTING A GOOD REED

As mentioned before, cane is a piece of wood and local temperature and humidity can and does affect the response of the reed. Try to eliminate, as much as possible, outside influences when selecting reeds for use in adjusting and playing. The following steps can be used in selecting reeds:

a. First, look for a nice shade of yellow in the bark. No dark spots or light areas.

b. Wet the butt end of the reed and if there is a tinge of green, the cane is not cured enough. Put the reed back in the box. It may cure in time.

c. Hold the reed up to the light and observe the fibers as they run to the tip. Is one side of the reed lighter in color? If so the reed is not balanced and very likely needs adjusting. Figure 3.

d. Look at the butt of the reed and see if the sides are even. Figure 3.

e. Check the sides of the reed and see if they are the same thickness. Figure 3.

If all of the above steps are followed, reeds will be found that need, with a proper breaking-in period, a minimum amount of adjusting.

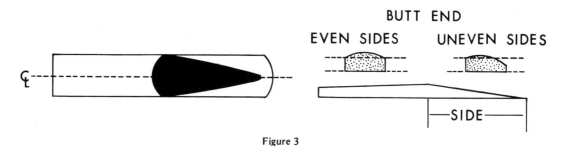

Figure 3

2. ADJUSTING REEDS

It is recommended that more than one reed be selected for future use. Reeds require a breaking-in period if they are to last and respond to the player's demands in making music. The breaking-in period will indicate what adjustments will have to be made to the reed, Students should not be allowed to play on reeds that are chipped, cracked, too soft or water soaked. Any of the former can cause embouchure changes that will require time to correct when playing on a good reed.

A. EQUIPMENT NEEDED WHEN ADJUSTING REEDS

Each student should have some basic equipment available to be used in adjusting and regulating reeds. The technique of adjusting reeds comes with practice. Success will depend on understanding some basic scrapes and polishes during the breaking in period. After all, time has been spent in selecting good reeds so a knowledge of adjustments will make that time pay off in reeds that will respond well and last longer. The following is a list of materials.

(1) A piece of glass approximately 4" x 4". This will be used as a flat surface for working on reeds as well as storing them during the breaking in period.

(2) Purchase a package of "Dutch Rush" from a music store. Rush will be used on wet reeds. Dutch Rush can be found along the shores of lakes with sandy beaches. Many times it is called "joint-grass".

(3) A sheet of No. 600 fine sandpaper or durite. (Available at lumberyards and hardware stores).

(4) A piece of brown wrapping paper 8" x 10" with no creases or wrinkles.

(5) Single edged razor blade and sharp pocket knife.

(6) Several large rubber bands. The rubber bands hold the reeds flat against the glass when they are drying out. This prevents the reeds from warping.

B. PROCEDURE FOR BREAKING IN AND ADJUSTING REEDS

Before wetting the reeds, take the sheet of brown wrapping paper and lay it on a flat hard surface, such as a table top or the top of a piano. IT MUST BE FLAT . . . NO BUMPS OR HUMPS. Place the fingers on the reed (Figure 4) and rub lightly back and forth several times with the grain of the reed. Now take a corner of the paper, wrap it over the index finger and rub the vamp of the reed. Figure 5. Polishing seals the open pores of the cane and prevents excess moisture from gathering in the body of the reed. The less excess moisture, the longer the reed will last.

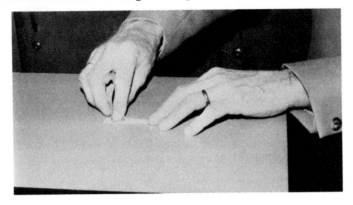

Figure 4

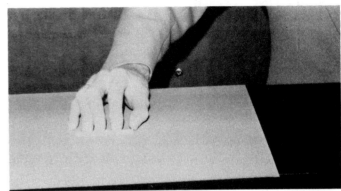

Figure 5

After sealing the reeds, place them in a glass of water to soak for a few minutes. Remove a reed, place it on the instrument and play for two or three minutes. Do the same with the rest of the reeds. Do not play on each reed too long as the embouchure will change or tire. Using a pencil, mark each reed with a code of some kind. For instance, H for hard, G for good, S for soft. The markings will give a clue when adjusting the reed. After playing and marking all the reeds, put them on the sheet of glass, secure them with the rubber bands and let them dry.

Repeat the process three or four days in a row. 1. Polish the reeds. 2. Soak the reeds. 3. Play and mark the reeds. All three steps are important. DO NOT SKIP OR OVERLOOK THESE STEPS.

C. ADJUSTING

Hold the reed up to the light. Observe the light and dark areas in the center, the sides and tip. Figure 6. 1. Good reed balanced on both sides. 2. The left side of the reed is not balanced with the right. 3. The right side is not balanced with the left. 4. The parts of the reed.

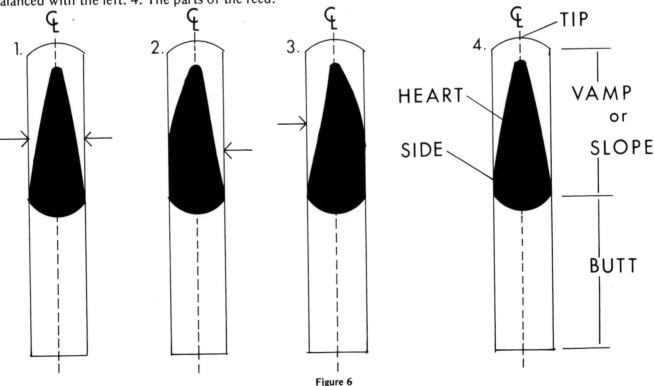

Figure 6

When adjusting a reed if it is wet, use Dutch Rush and if it is dry, use a small piece of fine sandpaper wrapped around the index finger.

(a) Rub the Dutch Rush or sandpaper along the dark side several times. Stay away from the center and the very tip of the reed. Use a curving motion. Figure 7.

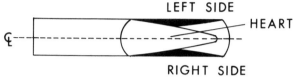

Figure 7

Hold the reed to the light and check for evenness of light on both sides of the reed. Try the reed to see if the response is better. If not, remove some more dark area. When the response improves, set the reed aside and check it the next day. Don't be in a hurry.

(b) If the reed looks balanced but still blows hard, remove some fibers on both sides of the reed. Chances are the sides are too thick. Remember, try the reed often and be patient.

(c) If reed continues to blow hard, after several sessions, lay the sandpaper on the piece of glass. Rub the reed gently across the paper in *ONE DIRECTION ONLY, NOT BACK AND FORTH!* Figure 8.

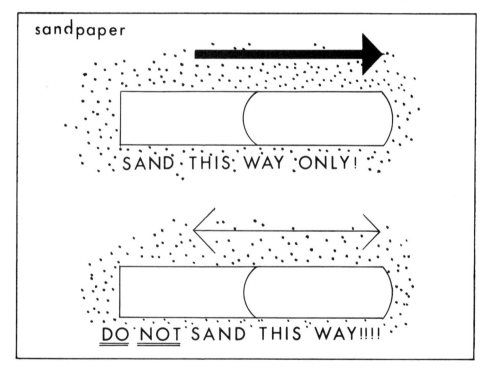

Figure 8

(d) The tip of the reed seldom needs work. Most of the time the tip will be too soft. Do not touch the tip until all of the above steps have been followed. The time to work on the tip, if work is needed, is during the final adjusting. Play a good solid crescendo and if you find the reed closing, remove it and clip a small amount from the tip. Reed clippers are available from your band director or may be purchased at a music store.

(e) Cut a groove through the bark even with the top of the ligature. Use the reed knife or jack knife. Figure 9.

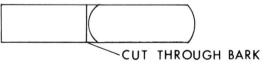

Figure 9

Check the reed and if it blows better but still not free enough, remove the bark ahead of the cut. Use the reed knife or jack knife. Remember to scrape with the blade. Don't carve with the knife. Figure 10.

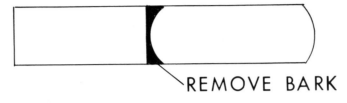

REMOVE BARK

Figure 10

(f) Have the *band director demonstrate* this next procedure. Lay the reed on the piece of glass. With the knife cut three or four grooves *through the bark*. Start at the butt and cut to the vamp. The grooves will improve the vibrations of the reed. Figure 11.

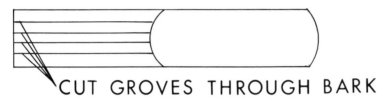

CUT GROVES THROUGH BARK

Figure 11

(g) Another delicate adjustment can be made with a single edge razor blade. *EXTREME CAUTION* must be used during this adjustment. Have a little container for the razor blade when in the case. Make several *LIGHT* scratch marks across the reed with the razor blade. The scratches are just deep enough to be seen by the eye. DO NOT MAKE SCRATCHES TO THE TIP OF THE REED. Figure 12.

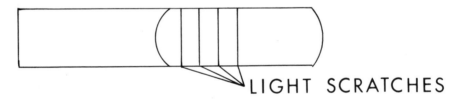

LIGHT SCRATCHES

Figure 12

As practice is gained in adjusting reeds, the student will find great satisfaction in playing on reeds that respond well. Take the time to build this skill.

D. LIGATURE, REED AND MOUTHPIECE ADJUSTMENTS

After selecting a good reed it is important that the reed be placed properly on the mouthpiece. 1. Wet the reed with water or saliva. Make sure all wrinkles are out of the tip. 2. Place the ligature on the mouthpiece with the screws loosened. 3. Slide the butt end of the reed under the ligature. 4. Position the reed so the sides and tip are even with the rails and tip of the mouthpiece. 5. Open the screws of the ligature more so the ligature can slide down away from the tip. Look for a line on the side of the mouthpiece. Place the top of the ligature just below the top line. 6. Using your right thumb, press the tip of the reed against the tip of the mouthpiece. A thin black line should appear through the tip of the reed. If not, adjust the reed until the black line is visible. 7. Make sure, and this is important, that the ligature is centered with the center of the reed. *Tighten the top screw very little,* just enough to keep the screw from backing out. The bottom screw can be tightened firmly but *not* so much that the metal is stretched. 8. The ligature is designed to hold the reed firmly with even pressure on the top of the reed. Excess pressure will affect the reed's response. 9. Treat the ligature with care. Prevent it from being damaged by overtightening or becoming bent. If this happens, replace the ligature. Many times, poor reed response can be traced to a ligature that has been stretched or bent by carelessness.

Unit III. Playing Position

The Alto Clarinet is usually played with a neck strap but today we are seeing more Alto Clarinets equipped with floor pegs. This trend is to be encouraged, as the floor peg is adjustable and the result is proper playing height and correct finger position. The young student is relieved of the heavy weight of the instrument on the neck and the right thumb. It will be much easier for the student to sit *erect* with both feet on the floor and with the back and shoulders pulled away from the back rest of the chair. If a floor peg is not used, be sure the student is sitting up straight and uses an adjustable NON-SLIP neck strap.

In any case, the playing position of the Alto Clarinet should not be on the right side of the body as recommended and observed by saxophone students. The Alto Clarinet neck-pipe and keys have been designed to be played as demonstrated in Figure 13.

Figure 13 (Front)

Figure 13 (Side)

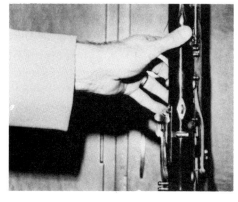

Figure 14

Refer to the pictures and observe the position of the left and right hands. Notice the position of the 1st finger left hand. See how it curves slightly and is in position to depress the G-sharp and A keys. This position is controlled by the thumb. The thumb should be at a 45 degree angle to the register key. Figure 14.

Notice the position of the head. It is upright. The head is not raised up or down but in a position so the eyes can look straight ahead.

Have a friend check body, hand and head position. If they do not look like the pictures: 1. If a floor peg is used, check for proper height. If a neck strap is used, check for slipping or perhaps the strap has been pulled too tight. 2. Is the body erect? 3. Is left thumb at the correct angle? 4. Is the head angle correct? Don't neglect any of the above check points. Proper playing positions are important to progress.

Unit IV. Embouchure and Mouthpiece Position

Most students are transfers from the B flat soprano clarinet and because of this proper embouchure formation is very important. Two differences are: 1. There is more pressure on the top of the mouthpiece from the top teeth than on the reed from the lower lip. 2. The angle of the mouthpiece as it enters the mouth must be correct. Recheck the correct height of the instrument as covered in "UNIT III".

Correct height controls the angle of the mouthpiece as it enters the mouth and equally important is the head position. If the student will remember the instrument *COMES TO YOU* and not the head and body to the instrument, they will find that a correct embouchure will be much easier to form and develop.

The mouthpiece is bigger than the soprano mouthpiece, so more mouthpiece is used in the mouth. Makes sense, doesn't it? The student should have enough mouthpiece in the mouth so that the lower lip is even with the *Resistance Curve.* This amount of mouthpiece will allow the lower lip to control the vibrations of the reed without interfering with the production of a good tone. Too little mouthpiece will produce a fuzzy, weak tone and may also produce squeaks.

A. FORMING THE EMBOUCHURE

The embouchure for the larger clarinets is referred to as the "Pucker" embouchure. The lower lip and chin muscles are not stretched as firm as on the soprano clarinet.

1. Look in a mirror and close the mouth naturally.

2. Now "pucker" the lips slightly. Notice in the center of the lower lips the lines that have formed.

3. Look at the chin and you will see the muscles and skin are *slightly* stretched. *Do not* bunch the chin muscles.

4. Keep the firm "pucker", blow a steady stream of air through the lips. Imagine that the air stream is trying to bend the flame of a lighted candle. Figure 15.

Figure 15

This is how a good embouchure should look and feel. It should have the feeling of a round "O". The corners of the mouth should feel as if they are pulled towards the sides of the mouthpiece. Think of a drawstring purse. The purse has two strings that are pulled to close the top of the purse. Imagine two strings around the lips. One end is hanging from the right side of the mouth and the other from the left side. While looking in the mirror, pull on the imaginary strings. Notice how the lips form a firm "pucker".

B. MOUTHPIECE POSITION

1. The mouthpiece should enter the mouth at a right angle to the body of the instrument. As the mouthpiece enters the mouth, a slight bit of the red on the lower lip will cover the lower teeth. It is important not too much

lower lip be over the lower teeth as that will dampen the vibrations of the reed.

2. Now place the upper teeth on the mouthpiece about where the resistance curve begins. Next drop the head *slightly* so the upper teeth push down gently on the mouthpiece. This action releases pressure on the reed by the lower lip and helps to form the "pucker".

The following exercise will help the student check for the correct amount of mouthpiece to be used in playing. Figure 16.

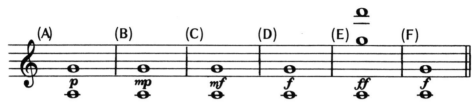

Figure 16

(a) Try the tip of the mouthpiece in the mouth. Tone will be soft, pinched and may squeak.

(b) Try a bit more mouthpiece in the mouth. Tone will begin to open but will lack body and resonance.

(c) Try a bit more mouthpiece. Tone will continue to grow in resonance and body.

(d) Try a bit more mouthpiece. Now the tone should have a nice round resonant sound with many overtones and a good center.

(e) Try a bit more. Clarinet tone may jump to the overtone or produce a harsh uncontrolled sound.

(f) Now back off a bit on the mouthpiece and the tone should sound as it did at letter (d).

(g) It is recommended the student include the above in his daily practice for several weeks after transferring. A serious player will continue, from time to time, to check on the above. There is a tendency to decrease the amount of mouthpiece in the mouth by all young students.

Unit V. Tuning and Intonation

The manufacturers of clarinets have tried, as much as possible, to develop a clarinet that will play in tune at 72 degrees Fahrenheit. So, if the instrument is cold it will play flat. Always warm the instrument by playing scales or long tones before tuning.

The clarinet has many parts that can and do affect intonation and tuning. The reed, ligature, mouthpiece, key adjustment and pad condition can and do affect intonation and tuning. So check these parts to make sure they are in proper working condition when tuning the instrument.

A. TUNING
The following notes are used to tune the clarinet. Figure 17.

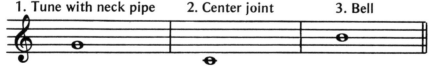

Figure 17

If the neck-pipe is pulled too much in tuning middle C or B natural third line, the throat tones will be very flat. Care must be taken in pulling the neck-pipe so these notes will not be affected. Pull enough to play the notes given in the exercise and the instrument will be equally stretched. Begin with the neck-pipe, then the middle joint and last the bell joint. If one of the above notes cannot be played in tune after pulling, a compromise will have to be made in all joints.

B. REED, EMBOUCHURE, MOUTHPIECE AND DYNAMICS AND THEIR EFFECT ON INTONATION

1. Reed — A reed that is too hard will have a tendency to make the instrument play sharp. A reed that is too soft or water soaked will have a tendency to play flat. As mentioned earlier, the student should have more than one reed ready to be used in playing.

2. Embouchure — Improper forming of the embouchure, not "puckered" enough, lower teeth biting lower lip, upper teeth not pushing down *gently* on the mouthpiece, not enough mouthpiece in the mouth, head position not correct, will affect the intonation of the instrument.

3. Mouthpiece — If a mouthpiece needs replacing, be sure to select one that matches the bore of the instrument. Some makes of mouthpieces are not interchangeable with all instruments. If the "lay" has been changed, medium to medium-open, for example, allow the student time to adjust to the change. Each mouthpiece requires individual reed adjustments to fit the "lay" and "tip opening". After the student has made the adjustment a correct decision can be made in the selection of a new mouthpiece.

4. Dynamics and Breath Control — Breath support and air stream controls the dynamic contrasts in music. If these are not well developed, pitch problems will result. It is human nature to bite on the mouthpiece when playing softly. It is the breath support and air stream with a slight relaxing of the embouchure that will play the note in tune. Using a tuner, the student should play an F Major scale slowly with the indicated dynamics. While playing, observe the pitch centers in the windows of the tuner. The pitch variations can be obserbed as the student tightens or loosens the embouchure. A rule of thumb is: the louder the note the firmer the embouchure. The softer the note the less firmness with good support. In other words, support and air stream play the notes in tune. Figure 18.

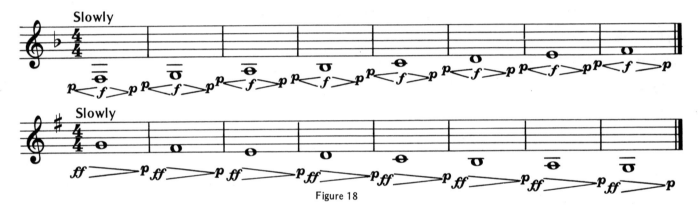

Figure 18

Unit VI. Breathing

All wind instruments require energy to make them sound. The clarinet is no exception. Energy of some kind must be created to make the reed vibrate. The physical effort used in inhaling and exhaling, with proper support, creates energy in the air stream as it sets the reed in motion. Many times pitch problems and poor tone quality can be traced to incorrect breath support. Students should spend time to develop correct breath support. Correct support cannot be neglected.

When filling the lungs there should be no raising of the shoulders. The waistline should expand outward. When exhaling the waistline and stomach should remain firm. This action allows the diaphragm to create pressure in the chest cavity, and this action creates energy in the air stream.

A. INHALING

Stand in front of a mirror. Put one hand on the abdomen. Close the mouth and inhale through the nose as though sniffing a flower. Take several sniffs and imagine the air is pushing out on the hand. This action fills the lungs and expands the waistline. DO NOT raise the shoulders.

B. EXHALING

Keep the waistline and stomach firm. Now "hiss" as loud as you can. Notice the air has pressure. DO NOT let the stomach become flabby or sink inward. Try the exercise again and hold the "hiss" as long as you can for several counts. When done correctly, the air stream will have point, pressure and energy.

The band or choir director can help with further suggestions and exercises in developing correct breathing habits. The large clarinets, because of their size, require more volume of air. Deep breathing and proper support are essential to successful playing. Proper embouchure and breath support are connected and should be thought of as combined and not as individual habits to be formed.

C. DEVELOPING LONG TONES

The following exercise has been designed to develop proper breath support. The student should follow the routine below: Figure 19.

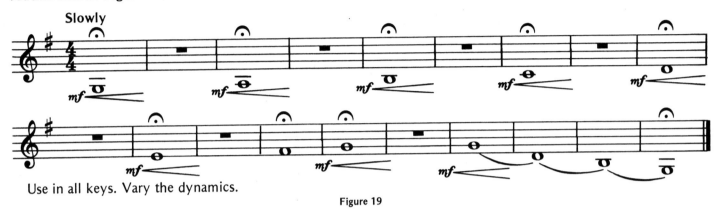

Use in all keys. Vary the dynamics.

Figure 19

1. Inhale, filling the lungs and expanding the waist.

2. Form the embouchure, and then put the mouthpiece in the mouth.

3. Start the air flow gently through the clarinet. Continue to expand the waist and abdomen while exhaling.

4. When the tone begins, increase the air pressure until a forte (*f*,) is reached. Hold the note four (4) slow counts.

5. While playing, check the embouchure and firmness of the waistline and abdomen.

6. Rest four (4) counts and repeat the routine.

Remember, to form a good embouchure, expand the waist and abdomen when inhaling and exhaling. Watch a little baby lying in its crib when crying. Notice how the stomach expands when inhaling and stays firm when crying. One can hear the energy in the sound. Right?

Unit VII. Tonguing

The tendency in tonguing, with a big mouthpiece and reed, is to slap the reed with the tongue or to use too much tongue surface on the reed when starting the tone. Now is the time to analyze how the tongue, breath support and air stream work together when articulating the length of notes when tonguing.

A. PLACEMENT OF THE TONGUE

1. Say the syllable "due" several times slowly.

2. Concentrate on that part of the tongue that touches the roof of the mouth.

3. Continue to say "due", touching the roof of the mouth as gently as possible.

4. That part and surface of the tongue is used to touch the reed as close to the tip as possible.

5. The tongue is a valve that starts and stops the air.

6. Think that part of the tongue is a feather as it touches the reed.

14

B. TONGUE ACTION

1. The air stream produces the tone so the tongue must not interfere with the air stream as it produces the tone. Place the tongue gently on the reed. Increase the breath support so the air stream is right behind the upper teeth. Remove the tongue and the air stream will start the note. REPEAT SEVERAL TIMES.

2. Different syllables are used when producing very little space, normal space, or lots of space between notes. Even though different syllables are used, the tongue action is light when touching the reed.

3. "Tah" is used when playing notes of normal space. Do not pump the breath but touch the reed lightly near the tip and release the tongue gently.

4. "Doo" or "Dah" or "Dee" are used when playing legato or connected notes. "Doo" in the low register. "Dah" in the middle register and "Dee" in the upper register. Again, do not pump the breath. Let the tongue touch the reed near the tip gently. The term for this style is "legato" or connected.

5. It is difficult to develop a short or "staccato" tongue on the larger clarinets. With a larger bore, bigger mouthpiece and reed, the response is slower than the soprano clarinet. However, it is possible to develop short or staccato style with practice.

Often staccato tonguing is played incorrectly. Most students play all staccato notes the same length. The dot over or under a note signifies one-half the value of the note. The player has to think of two things when playing staccato: 1. Tempo of the selection. 2. The note value being played.

The syllable "Too" or "Tah" is used to play short or staccato notes.

Legato or Connected Tonguing Exercises

1. Slowly — Legato Tongue, very little space between notes. Use the syllable "Doo".

2. Slowly — Legato or Connected Style, the tongue is a feather. *DO NOT* pump the breath. Use the syllable "Due".

3. Slowly — Legato, use this exercise as new scales are introduced.

Use the above pattern on every scale degree in all keys.

1. A good *staccato* tongue cannot be developed without having a good *legato* tongue.

2. The notes should flow into each other with very little interruption of the sound.

3. Excellent studies can be found in the individual books that are part of the "Contemporary Band Method".

Normal or Spaced Tonguing Exercises

1. Moderate Tempo — Use "Tah" for normal tonguing and space between notes.

2. Moderatly Slow Tempo — Normal tonguing. *DO NOT* pump the breath. Use the syllable "Tah".

3. Moderatly Slow Tempo — Normal tonguing. *DO NOT* change the embouchure. Use the syllable "Tah".

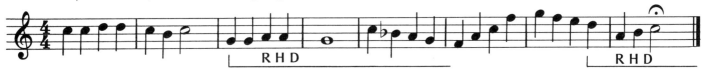

4. Normal Tonguing. Use the syllable "Tah".

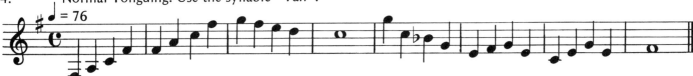

1. Sound the notes their full value.

2. Remember the tongue is a valve.

3. Breath support and a light tongue is the key to proper space between notes.

Staccato or Short Tonguing Exercises

Too often staccato tonguing is misunderstood. Most students play all staccato notes the same length no matter what the tempo of the selection might be. The dot over or under a note means one-half the value of the note. The player has to think of two things when playing staccato. 1. Tempo of the selection. 2. The value of the note being played at that tempo.

1a. Very Slow Tempo — Use the syllable "Too".

1b. Very Slow Tempo — Staccato — Should sound like 1a.

After playing several times, increase the tempo slightly. Do Not forget to count. Listen for the rests. Play notes full value. Stop the note with the tongue. Keep breath support on and air stream behind the teeth.

2. Moderate Tempo — Use the syllable "Too". Last 4 bars should sound the same as the 1st 4 bars.

3a. ♩= 60 — Short tonguing. Use the syllable "Too"

3b.

Did 3a sound like 3b? If not, repeat 3a and count the beats and rests. The beats have sound and the rests are silent.

REVIEW: Staccato is division. One half the value of the note plus tempo determins how long a note sounds when playing staccato. The slower the tempo the longer the note. The faster the tempo the shorter the note. THE AIR STREAM SHOULD BE RIGHT BEHIND THE TEETH. THE TONGUE IS USED LIGHTLY TO START AND STOP THE NOTE WHEN PLAYING STACCATO. THE BREATH IS NEVER PUMPED. AIR PRESSURE REMAINS CONSTANT.

Unit VIII. Tone Quality

Developing the aural concept of what is a good tone, requires the student to be exposed to good sounds that can be absorbed and imitated. All students should have at their disposal recordings by outstanding soloists. Another source is attendance at contests and festivals. Imitation is a very good teacher if used properly.

Tone quality is more than producing sound on an instrument. The tone must have vitality, resonance, be in tune and controlled. When the quality is of the best, the student should feel the vibrations in the instrument as well as in the mouth cavity. It is a living thing.

Tone quality cannot be developed by playing fast. A slow tempo allows the performer time to listen to each note and make the necessary wind, mouth cavity, tongue and embouchure adjustments. When these adjustments are practiced slowly, note by note, they become a part of the playing habits and will automatically be used at faster tempos.

It is assumed the instrument is in good mechanical condition, the reed has been properly adjusted, the breath support is correct and the proper mental attitude is brought to the practice session.

Try these short studies and follow the directions carefully.

Tone Building Exercises

1. Very Slowly — Move fingers in time with the music. 2. Do not change the embouchure.

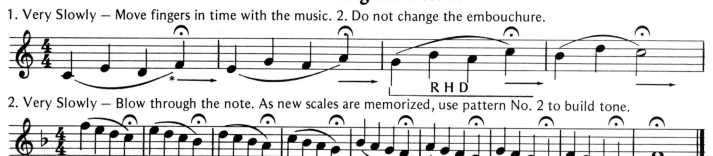

2. Very Slowly — Blow through the note. As new scales are memorized, use pattern No. 2 to build tone.

3. Very Slowly — First time through tongue in position of "Hah". Second time through *8va* higher. Tongue in the position of "Hee". Use No. 3 as new chromatic scales are introduced.

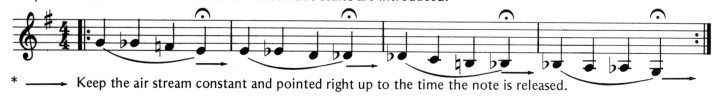

* ——→ Keep the air stream constant and pointed right up to the time the note is released.

Unit IX. Range

In recent years instrument manufacturers have been able to take advantage of many new metal alloys for keys and posts. These new alloys allow them to manufacture keys, pad cups and key posts that are lighter and more positive in their action. In addition to the new alloys, recent discoveries in acoustics affecting tone hole placement have allowed the manufacture to develop and produce an instrument that responds quickly to the players demands. So now we discover parts being written that require an extended range. Many notes and passages that were difficult to play in the past are no longer thought to be difficult for the young student. When the student has developed a good solid low register, it is time to extend the playing range. When taken one step at a time and practiced slowly, the student will be prepared to play in the "Clarion" and "Altissimo" registers when called upon to do so.

The following exercises should be practiced slowly and many times. Follow the directions and concentrate during the practice periods. It is recommended the student be referred to the *Supplemental Instrumental Methods* published by *Belwin-Mills Publishing Corp.* to further reinforce these studies.

Registers of the Clarinet

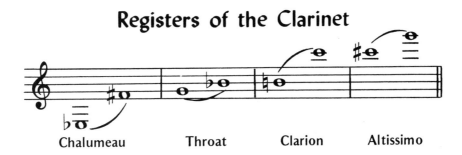

1. Open the register key gently.

Use the syllable "Tee" for correct tongue placement.
*Use the same finger pattern as in No. 3.

EL 2702

5. Slowly

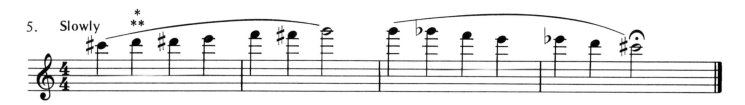

Use the syllable "Tee" with no embouchure change and a very light wind stream.
*Add E-flat little finger right hand for notes beginning with high D.
**Do not raise 1st finger left hand but slide it down to open little hole on the flat key.

6.

7.

Unit X. Practicing

A specific time each day should be set aside for the private practice period. It is only through constant attention to playing problems that one can make steady and continued progress. It is important to free this period of distractions. It is also important that the practice period establish the proper mental and physical attitudes in the student. Proper playing habits come only with concentration and attention to detail. The purpose of practicing is not to put in so many minutes each day but to make those minutes productive in every sense of the word.

Time must be spent during the first part of the period to warm up the mind, body and instrument. Makes sense, doesn't it? Warming up means warming the instrument, establishing the proper embouchure, breath support, and the mental and physical attitudes that will make the practice period a successful and satisfying experience. Tone building exercises or scales can be used during this segment of the practice period. These exercises or studies should be played slowly and the student should listen carefully to each note for clarity and balance, taking the time to correct poor sounding notes, embouchure formation, breath support and posture. Warming up is the preparation for the race or second part of the practice period. A swimmer or a long distance runner does not go all out when first entering the pool or the track. He takes the time to warm up the body and mind before the race or practice period.

The second part of the practice period should be devoted to the assigned study, scale or etude. The student should take time to study the music before playing, checking the key signature, time signature, fingerings, rhythmic problems, tempo and dynamic markings.

When a problem is discovered, attack the problem first before playing through the scale, study or etude. Play through the problem measure or measures slowly and carefully until the problem has been solved. Remember slow practice and concentration will build playing skills. When the problem has been solved, increase the tempo to the proper speed. DON'T PRACTICE YOUR MISTAKES, BUT RATHER CORRECT YOUR MISTAKES.

The third part of the practice period is the review period. Review a previous study, etude or scale. Treat this as the fun period. Continue to concentrate and play it better than the last time.

The fourth part of the practice period should be used to prepare and break in new reeds. Five minutes of every practice period should be devoted to this important skill. If this is done, the student will always have a good reed available.

How much time should one practice is a question that always arises. Thirty minutes a day used wisely by the young student will be very productive. However, at first the young student may find the muscles in the corners of the mouth aching. It is wise to stop and rest these muscles. While waiting for the muscles to recover use the time to adjust reeds or study a fingering or rhythm problem in the music. With continued practice these muscles will strengthen and the practice period can be lengthened.

Unit XI. Selected Etudes

1. Play slowly several times using indicated fingerings. Then, increase the tempo.

2. Same as No. 1.

3. Moderate tempo — Listen for eveness of finger movement.

4. Moderato — Do not be in a hurry. Lift first note into second note.

5. Slowly — Tone builders in Clarion Register.

* Chromatic fingering

EL 2702

6. Slowly — Normal tonguing. Move fingers evenly.

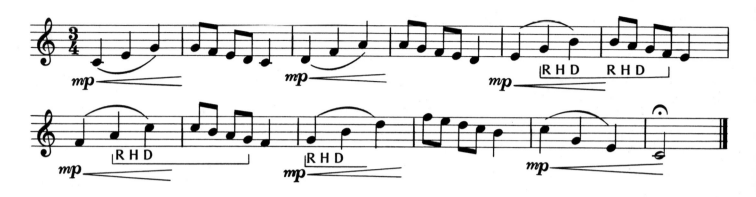

7. Moderato — Normal Tonguing. Move fingers with the pulse.

8. Legato tonguing.

9. Moderato — Normal tonguing. Play evenly and listen for tone.

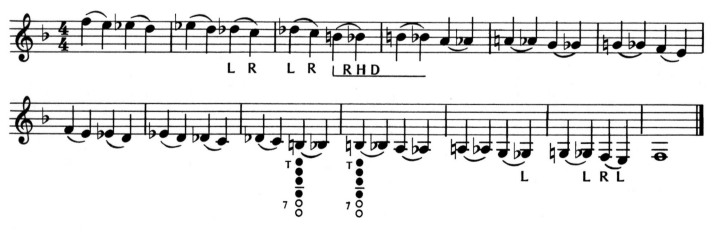

10. Moderato — Chromatic fingering check.

* Chromatic fingering

1. Slur first time then try these articulations.

2. RHD — keep right hand down.

11. Slowly — full and round tone.

12. Slowly and increase tempo.

13. Moderato.

14. Even steady tempo.

15. Slowly — legato tongue — connect the pitches.

16. Slowly — light tongue on the reed.

17. Moderato — do not rush.

EL 2702

FINGERING CHART
How To Read The Chart

● — Indicates hole closed, or keys to be pressed.

o — Indicates hole open.

When a number is given, refer to the picture of the Clarinet for additional key to be pressed.

When two notes are given together (F♯ and G♭), they are the same tone and, of course, played the same way.

When there are two fingerings given for a note, use the first one unless your teacher tells you otherwise.

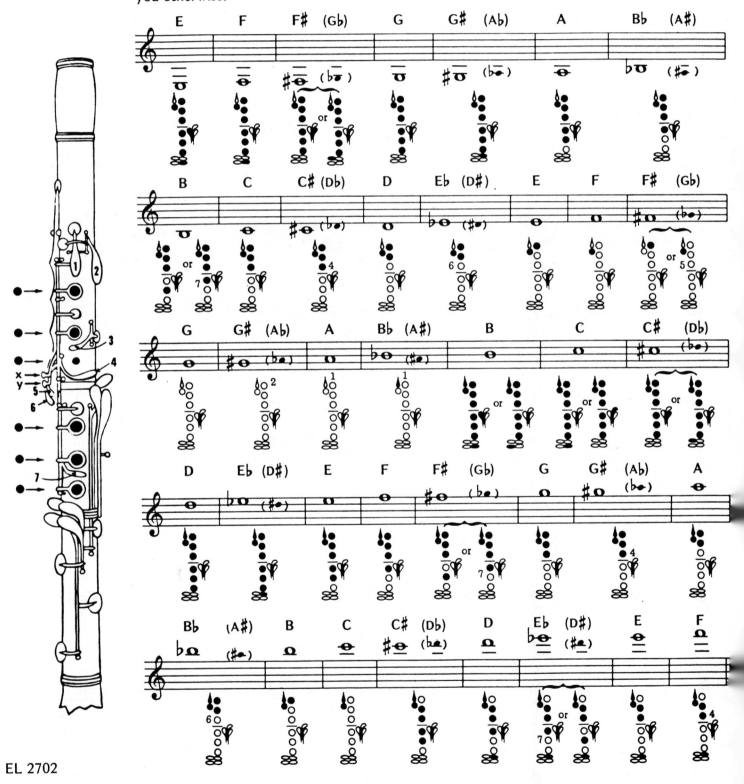